COMPANION WORKBOOK

Budget and Pay for Travel Using Points, Miles, and Other Rewards

HOW TO PLAN A FREE

THEME PARK VACATION

H. KINNEY

Copyright © 2022 H. Kinney

All rights reserved. No part of this book may be reproduced, stored in a retrieval system, distributed, or transmitted in any form or by any means, including photocopying, recording, or other electronic or mechanical methods, without prior written permission of the copyright owner except for the use of brief quotations in a book review. The advice and strategies found within may not be suitable for every situation. This book is for informational purposes only and is not professional financial advice. Neither the author, nor the publisher, assumes any responsibility or liability on behalf of the consumer or reader of this material. For permission requests, contact heidi@heidikinney.com.

ISBN: 978-1-7372557-9-6

Contents

My Ideal Theme Park Vacation	1
Trip Budget (Cash Cost)	3
Trip Budget (Rewards)	4
Theme Park Vacation Information	5
Free Theme Park Vacation Plan	7
Rewards Plan By Month	9
Rewards Tracker	17
Credit Card Tracker	19
Shopping Portal Tracker	21
Gift Cards Tracker	25
Cash Tracker	27
Lodging Comparison	29
Credit Card Comparison	31
Bank Account Comparison	35
Credit Card Annual Fee Analyzer	37
Shopping Portal Information	38
Notes	42
Author's Note	53

My Ideal Theme Park Vacation

Visualize your ideal theme park vacation. Then answer the questions.

Where will I go? _____
_____

How long will I stay? _____

Will anyone travel with me? _____
_____
_____
_____

When will I travel? (Month/Year) _____

Which theme park(s) will I visit? _____
_____
_____
_____
_____
_____

How many days will I spend at the park(s)? _____
_____
_____
_____

Will I visit anywhere besides the theme park(s)? _____
_____
_____
_____
_____

How will I get to my destination? _____
_____
_____

Will I need a rental car? _____

How close to the theme park will I stay? _____
_____
_____
_____

What hotel features and amenities do I want/need? _____
_____
_____
_____
_____
_____
_____

Will I stay at the same hotel for the entire length of the trip? _____
_____
_____

What types of dining experiences do I want? _____
_____
_____
_____

What else do I want to experience during the trip? _____
_____
_____
_____

Trip Budget (Cash Cost)

Research and estimate the cash cost of each item. Include fees, if applicable.

	Airline Option 1	Airline Option 2	Airline Option 3	Airport Transfers
TRANSPORTATION	Airfare	Airfare	Airfare	Parking
	Taxes & Fees	Taxes & Fees	Taxes & Fees	Rental Car
	Luggage	Luggage	Luggage	Gas & Tolls
	Total	Total	Total	Other
	Estimated Total Cost for Transportation:			

	Hotel Option 1	Hotel Option 2	Hotel Option 3
LODGING	Room Cost	Room Cost	Room Cost
	Taxes & Fees	Taxes & Fees	Taxes & Fees
	Other	Other	Other
	Total	Total	Total
	Estimated Total Cost for Lodging:		

	Park Tickets Option 1	Park Tickets Option 2	Park Tickets Option 3
OTHER	Meals & Snacks	Souvenirs	Other
	Estimated Total Cost for Other:		

Estimated Total Value of Theme Park Vacation:

Trip Budget (Rewards)

Research the rewards cost for each budget item, or write the cash cost.

TRANSPORTATION

Airline Option 1	Airline Option 2	Airline Option 3	Airport Transfers
Airfare	Airfare	Airfare	Parking
Taxes & Fees	Taxes & Fees	Taxes & Fees	Rental Car
Luggage	Luggage	Luggage	Gas & Tolls
			Other
Estimated Rewards Needed for Transportation:			

LODGING

Hotel Option 1	Hotel Option 2	Hotel Option 3
Room Cost	Room Cost	Room Cost
Taxes & Fees	Taxes & Fees	Taxes & Fees
Other	Other	Other
Estimated Rewards Needed for Lodging:		

OTHER

Park Tickets Option 1	Park Tickets Option 2	Park Tickets Option 3
Meals & Snacks	Souvenirs	Other
Estimated Rewards Needed for Other:		

Theme Park Vacation Information

Use these pages to record the important details of your vacation plan.

Destination: _____
_____
_____

Travel Dates: _____
_____
_____

Names of Travelers: _____
_____
_____
_____
_____
_____

Theme Park(s): _____
_____
_____
_____
_____

Other Places to Visit: _____
_____
_____
_____
_____
_____
_____

Transportation Plan & Info:

Lodging Plan & Info:

Dining Plan & Info:

Free Theme Park Vacation Plan

		Rewards Amount & Type Needed	Earn By Date	Date Earned	Date Redeemed
TRANSPORTATION	Airfare				
	Taxes & Fees				
	Luggage				
	Airport Transfers				
	Parking				
	Rental Car				
	Gas & Tolls				
	Other				
LODGING	Hotel Room				
	Taxes & Fees				
	Other				
OTHER	Park Tickets				
	Meals & Snacks				
	Souvenirs				
	Other				

How I Will Earn Rewards

Rewards Plan By Month

Use these pages to map out your rewards earning plan.

Month:
Research:
Join Rewards Program(s):
Open Account(s):
Earn:
Redeem:
Notes:

Month:
Research:
Join Rewards Program(s):
Open Account(s):
Earn:
Redeem:
Notes:

Month:
Research:
Join Rewards Program(s):
Open Account(s):
Earn:
Redeem:
Notes:

Month:
Research:
Join Rewards Program(s):
Open Account(s):
Earn:
Redeem:
Notes:

Month:
Research:
Join Rewards Program(s):
Open Account(s):
Earn:
Redeem:
Notes:

Month:
Research:
Join Rewards Program(s):
Open Account(s):
Earn:
Redeem:
Notes:

Month:
Research:
Join Rewards Program(s):
Open Account(s):
Earn:
Redeem:
Notes:

Month:
Research:
Join Rewards Program(s):
Open Account(s):
Earn:
Redeem:
Notes:

Month:
Research:
Join Rewards Program(s):
Open Account(s):
Earn:
Redeem:
Notes:

Month:
Research:
Join Rewards Program(s):
Open Account(s):
Earn:
Redeem:
Notes:

Month:
Research:
Join Rewards Program(s):
Open Account(s):
Earn:
Redeem:
Notes:

Month:
Research:
Join Rewards Program(s):
Open Account(s):
Earn:
Redeem:
Notes:

Month:
Research:
Join Rewards Program(s):
Open Account(s):
Earn:
Redeem:
Notes:

Month:
Research:
Join Rewards Program(s):
Open Account(s):
Earn:
Redeem:
Notes:

Month:
Research:
Join Rewards Program(s):
Open Account(s):
Earn:
Redeem:
Notes:

Month:
Research:
Join Rewards Program(s):
Open Account(s):
Earn:
Redeem:
Notes:

Month:
Research:
Join Rewards Program(s):
Open Account(s):
Earn:
Redeem:
Notes:

Month:
Research:
Join Rewards Program(s):
Open Account(s):
Earn:
Redeem:
Notes:

Month:
Research:
Join Rewards Program(s):
Open Account(s):
Earn:
Redeem:
Notes:

Month:
Research:
Join Rewards Program(s):
Open Account(s):
Earn:
Redeem:
Notes:

Month:
Research:
Join Rewards Program(s):
Open Account(s):
Earn:
Redeem:
Notes:

Month:
Research:
Join Rewards Program(s):
Open Account(s):
Earn:
Redeem:
Notes:

Month:
Research:
Join Rewards Program(s):
Open Account(s):
Earn:
Redeem:
Notes:

Month:
Research:
Join Rewards Program(s):
Open Account(s):
Earn:
Redeem:
Notes:

Rewards Tracker

Rewards Program	January	February	March	April	May	June

July	August	September	October	November	December	Notes/Expiration

Credit Card Tracker

Card Name	Issuer	Application Date	Rewards Type	Earnings Rate	Rewards Value	Annual Fee

Bonus Terms	Estimated Bonus Value	Bonus Met	Bonus Posted	Redemption Plan

Shopping Portal Tracker

Date	Store	Portal	Rate	Purchase Amount	Rewards Expected	Rewards Posted	Notes

Date	Store	Portal	Rate	Purchase Amount	Rewards Expected	Rewards Posted	Notes

Date	Store	Portal	Rate	Purchase Amount	Rewards Expected	Rewards Posted	Notes

Date	Store	Portal	Rate	Purchase Amount	Rewards Expected	Rewards Posted	Notes

Gift Cards Tracker

Date	Gift Card	Amount	Cost/Source	Planned Use

Date	Gift Card	Amount	Cost/Source	Planned Use

Cash Tracker

Date	Amount	Source	Planned Use	Balance

Date	Amount	Source	Planned Use	Balance

Lodging Comparison

	Lodging			
Type				
Location				
Room Rate (Cash)				
Room Rate (Rewards)				
Resort Fee				
Parking Fee				
Amenities				
Dining Options				
Rewards Program				
Status Perks				
Other				

	Lodging			
Type				
Location				
Room Rate (Cash)				
Room Rate (Rewards)				
Resort Fee				
Parking Fee				
Amenities				
Dining Options				
Rewards Program				
Status Perks				
Other				

Credit Card Comparison

	Credit Card			
Issuer				
Annual Fee				
Rewards Type				
Rewards Value				
Current Bonus				
Value of Bonus				
Minimum Spend Requirement				
Best Historical Bonus				
Earnings Rate				
Card Benefits				
Redemption Options				

	Credit Card			
Issuer				
Annual Fee				
Rewards Type				
Rewards Value				
Current Bonus				
Value of Bonus				
Minimum Spend Requirement				
Best Historical Bonus				
Earnings Rate				
Card Benefits				
Redemption Options				

	Credit Card			
Issuer				
Annual Fee				
Rewards Type				
Rewards Value				
Current Bonus				
Value of Bonus				
Minimum Spend Requirement				
Best Historical Bonus				
Earnings Rate				
Card Benefits				
Redemption Options				

	Credit Card			
Issuer				
Annual Fee				
Rewards Type				
Rewards Value				
Current Bonus				
Value of Bonus				
Minimum Spend Requirement				
Best Historical Bonus				
Earnings Rate				
Card Benefits				
Redemption Options				

Bank Account Comparison

	Bank			
Name				
Account Type				
Interest Rate				
Minimum Deposit				
Minimum Balance				
Fees & Ways to Avoid Them				
Bonus				
Bonus Terms				
Best Historical Bonus				
Account Benefits				
Notes				

	Bank			
Name				
Account Type				
Interest Rate				
Minimum Deposit				
Minimum Balance				
Fees & Ways to Avoid Them				
Bonus				
Bonus Terms				
Best Historical Bonus				
Account Benefits				
Notes				

Credit Card Annual Fee Analyzer

Use this form to help you decide if a credit card's annual fee is worth paying.

		Credit Card				
Annual Fee						
Welcome Bonus						
Rewards Type						
Rewards Value						
Earnings Rate						
Redemption Options						
CARD BENEFITS AND THEIR VALUE TO ME	Benefit:					
	Value to Me					
	Benefit					
	Value to Me					
	Benefit					
	Value to Me					
	Benefit					
	Value to Me					
	Benefit					
	Value to Me					
	Total Value of Benefits to Me					
Year 1 Total Value of Benefits Plus Value of Welcome Bonus Minus Annual Fee						
Years 2+ Total Value of Benefits Minus Annual Fee						
Worth the fee?						

Shopping Portal Information

Name	New User Bonus & Terms	Redemption Minimum	Redemption Methods	App	Inactivity Fee	Joined

Notes

Author's Note

If you enjoyed using the *How to Plan a Free Theme Park Vacation Companion Workbook*, please help others find this book by leaving a review where you purchased it. Thank you!

Visit heidikinney.com/freevacation for helpful links and resources.

To plan and organize the other details of your trip, consider these books.
Theme Park Vacation Planner, Weekend Edition
Theme Park Vacation Planner, One-Week Edition
Theme Park Vacation Planner, Two-Week Edition
Pocket-Sized Theme Park Vacation Planner, Weekend Edition
Pocket-Sized Theme Park Vacation Planner, One-Week Edition
Pocket-Sized Theme Park Vacation Planner, Two-Week Edition

www.ingramcontent.com/pod-product-compliance
Lightning Source LLC
Chambersburg PA
CBHW081628100526
44590CB00021B/3647